WILDLIFE
OF THE
ROCKY
MOUNTAINS

Developed and produced by

John Hinde Curteich Inc.

Westlake Village, California 91362

Written and edited by Lucy Hanley

Art director and design by Beatriz G. Mojarro

While every care is taken in compiling this book,

no responsibility can be taken for errors or omissions.

Front Cover: All animals by Stan Osolinski except Golden Eagle, Richard Strange; Landscape, John Hinde Curteich.

Back Cover: Stan Osolinski

81IRM-1

WILDLIFE OF THE ROCKY MOUNTAINS

Contents

Preface 4

Diversity 5

Adaptation .6

Balance of Nature and the Food Chain . . .7

Survival of the Fittest 8

Hoofed Mammals 9

Elk 10-12		Bison 17-18
Bull Moose 13-14		Pronghorn Antelope 19-20
Mule Deer 15-16		Mountain (Bighorn) Sheep 21-22
White-tailed Deer 16		Mountain Goat 23

Carnivores 24

Grizzly Bear 25-27		Bobcat .34
Black Bear 28		Red Fox 35
Gray Wolf 29-30		Badger .36
Mountain Lion 31		Raccoon 36
Coyote 32-33		River Otter 37
Lynx 34		Long-tailed Weasel 37

Gnawing Mammals 38

Prairie Dog 39		Golden-mantled Ground Squirrel 43
Porcupine 40		Least Chipmunk 44
Beaver .41		Uinta Ground Squirrel 45
Yellow-bellied Marmot 42		Abert's Squirrel 46

Birds 47

Bald Eagle 48-49		Canada Geese 57-58
Golden Eagle 50		Mallard Ducks 59
Great Gray Owl 51		Ruffed Grouse 60
Osprey .52		Blue Grouse 60
Raven .53		Wild Turkey 61
Yellow-headed Blackbird 53		Mountain Bluebird 62
Stellar Jay 54		White-tailed Ptarmigan 63
White Pelican 55		Sandhill Crane 64
Trumpeter Swans 56		

PREFACE

Nothing is so awesome as to contemplate that we, mankind, the dominant species, share the earth with all kinds of creatures, great and small, who live and play, work and reproduce, raise their young and die...just as we do...all within our domain to observe and appreciate. The panoramic Rocky Mountains, with their majestic size and scale and their many still-wild places, contain spectacular scenery and provide a showcase for wildlife. Much of the area is set aside by law to be preserved in its natural state for public education and recreation. There are several national parks in the range, including the oldest and largest, Yellowstone National Park, established in 1872, with 3,472 square miles of unspoiled wonderland. Additionally, many of the country's 450 national wildlife refuges are located within the Rocky Mountains.

In God's wilderness is the hope of the world The great fresh, unblighted, unredeemed wilderness.

....John Muir (1838-1914)

Straddling the crest of the continent, the great Rockies are a geologic chronicle to the Precambrian past when the forces of fire, ice, wind and water, began to carve the landscape and build the mountains as we see them today. When we explore these magnificent vistas of mountains, valleys and forests, we are moving among the remnants of creation that began nearly five billion years ago. Within this depth of field, from here to infinity, man is a visitor; but he does not have to be a stranger.

iverse as the landscape itself. The mountains ary from majestically sculptured towering peaks o deeply etched lake-filled valleys; from flower- blanketed meadows to lush green forest slopes; from rich red canyon sands to blue-tinted alpine glaciers. This dramatic environment provides home and shelter to an abundance of wildlife. The animals vary from the lowly earth-bound ant o the lofty sky-soaring eagle; from the crowd- friendly ground squirrel to the grizzly bear; from he tender, doe-eyed deer to the deadly swift mountain lion.

A great upheaval of earth's crust and periods of geologic activity, including massive sculpting by glaciers, shaped the landscape that we call the Rocky Mountains. Beginning in Northern New Mexico, the mountain chain extends as far north as Alaska. This great range stretches across Arizona, Utah, Colorado, Nevada, Wyoming, daho and Montana; then passes the international border, extending through the Canadian provinces

Territories and Yukon Territory. As the mountains continue beyond Alaska, they gradually disappear into a series of ice covered hills at the Arctic Circle.

Mountain regions vary greatly because o latitude, elevation, climate, and soil conditions Within the Rockies, climates extend from the northern fringe of the subtropical zone in the far south to the Arctic in the far north. The altitude of timberline decreases as latitude increases There are three major life zones. The relatively warm and dry lowest vegetation belt is called the Montane Zone. Above the foothills but below the tree line is the Canadian or Subalpine Zone ir which the rigors of harsh climate are visible. The elevation where trees cease to grow is called the Alpine Zone, which features barren tundra with severe winter conditions and short, cold summers Some peaks remain snow-covered year round while many high valleys support permanen glaciers. Only the heartiest creatures survive these conditions. The wilderness of the Rocky Mountains is not one, but many wildernesses.

ADAPTATION

In order to exist and propagate their species, all living things must find food, protect themselves and reproduce their kind. Adaptations to their environments are the principal ways that plants and animals solve challenges of staying alive. Individuals may adapt within their lifetimes, but the species adapts gradually over several generations if it is to survive. Plants and animals that have the greatest powers of adaptation to changing living conditions are the ones that have evolved to thrive today.

Unlike plants that can manufacture their own food, animals must develop special organs and skills for finding food. For instance, the hoofs of mountain mammals evolved from toes into a divided cleft which provides strong tools for elk, deer, sheep and goats to dig for food in the wild, or kick through snow to the frozen ground for grass in winter. Another example is the grizzly bear that digs for roots and bulbs, or rodents in their burrows, to satisfy its mighty appetite. To accommodate this specialty, the grizzly's claws

have adapted by growing longer, stronger and straighter than smaller bears with less voracious appetites.

Likewise, the flat upper teeth of hoofed animals are well adapted to chewing and grinding leafy foods, whereas the sharp incisors of carnivores (meat-eating animals) are specialized for ripping and tearing flesh. The beaver's large and strong teeth are highly specialized for gnawing through tree trunks. Birds do not have teeth, but have beaks that are adapted to specific food-hunting jobs such as chiseling, boring, spearing, and cracking. Even birds' feet have adapted to specific needs of individuals. For example, perching birds have toes that clamp around a branch to keep them from falling off, while woodpeckers have sharp, curved claws to climb and cling onto the trunk of a tree. Big birds of prey, like eagles and hawks, have sharp, curved claws to catch and grasp their victims and hold them while carrying them away.

BALANCE OF NATURE AND THE FOOD CHAIN

Plants and animals serve man to provide food, textiles, building materials and many useful products. However, the most important service that animals provide to man is their role in the balance of nature. Plants and animals coexist in a symbiotic relationship, often called the web of life. This intricate system revolves around a cycle in which animals help build life by serving as food to man and plants, but animals also destroy life by eating other animals and plants. Much of the food thus eaten is returned to earth to feed plants in the form of bodily wastes or bodily decay, after death. Thus, in nature, nothing is wasted.

The laws of nature require that animals must eat plants as well as hunt and kill each other, so that the total number of plants and animals is held in balance. If the population of a species becomes too large for the existing food supply, the species cannot thrive and the group will gradually decline. When overpopulation occurs, the range deteriorates. In time, the inferior population is destined to survive on scanty rations and to grow weak and die in severe winters. Predators, such as the mountain lion, the wolf and the grizzly bear, help preserve the balance of nature by keeping the deer and elk population in check. However, a recurring problem in the Rockies is that elk herds have multiplied too greatly because there are relatively few large predators remaining to hunt them.

If the food chain is disturbed anywhere along the line, all living things within the chain are affected. For example, mites eat plants; bugs eat mites; birds eat bugs; snakes eat birds; bigger birds eat snakes and so on. Each species has its natural enemies. Within this vital inter-dependent relationship, the chain is as strong as its weakest link.

SURVIVAL
OF THE FITTEST

Nature is a great and generous teacher, but she is thrifty; she wastes nothing. In the vast wilderness of the Rocky Mountains, as in every other habitat of the world, resources are limited. There is not enough food, water, shelter or space for the offspring of all plants and animals. In the fierce struggle for life, plants and animals compete for limited necessities. Some are better suited than others are for this challenge. Gradually, over time, adaptations occur and the favored species survives. This process is called natural selection or survival of the fittest.

In nature there are neither rewards nor punishments— there are consequences.

...R.G. Ingersoll (1833-99)

Among many species, males compete for the right to reproduce. In this mating rivalry, the younger, stronger, smarter male usually wins. Thus, offspring are born with a better chance for survival. In spite of this genetic head start, many infants do not survive. Unhatched eggs and live young are prime food sources for other animals. Almost from the moment of conception, new organisms enter the food chain.

For those plants and animals that survive infancy, ultimately, which will live and which will die is determined by how well they compete for limited resources. On the whole, the fittest will survive.

HOOFED MAMMALS

Over sixty species of mammals live in the Rockies. The bison, often called the American buffalo, is the largest animal at an average of 2,000 pounds. In the mid-19th century, about twenty million of these animals thundered over the western plains and mountain meadowlands, but by the end of the century, the species had been hunted to near extinction. Likewise, the pronghorn species, often called antelope, nearly perished due to of overhunting. Today, because of game laws and other protective measures, both species are making a comeback.

Wapiti (elk), deer, moose and caribou, all members of the deer family, are the most common large animals in the Rockies. The largest of these is the moose, which weighs up to 1,400 pounds. During the summer, bull moose are often found knee-deep in water, eating over 100 pounds of aquatic forage each day. Like a prizefighter preparing for the ring, the moose is "beefing-up" for the ritual rut. Concurrently, elk are grazing and browsing in the grasslands to add weight for their courtship struggles. Meanwhile, high in the alpine meadows, bighorn sheep and mountain goats are also busy adding body fat to prepare for mating and for winter.

In the fall, male members of the deer family rub the velvet from their bone-hard antlers and are ready for the mating tussles. Courting rituals are similar for all hoofed animals. During the rut, the hills and valleys echo with primordial mating calls and spine-chilling crashes of horns. The bull elk, which averages 1,000 pounds in weight, gathers a group of cows, circles the perimeter and bugles his loud resonate call to intimidate approaching aggressors. Male rivals charge at each other and wield their mighty antlers in a machismo contest of strength. The antagonists butt horns and try to outpush each other. The superior bull usually wins and earns the right to take several cows for his mates. An exceptional bull may take a harem of 60 cows or more, but the average bull keeps only a dozen or so.

In a nearly identical drama, bighorn sheep come down from the high country to their breeding grounds. The male ram's horns grow in a half circle alongside his head and can reach a spiraled length of four feet. The bigger the horns, the more dominant the animal. When two rams go head to head, the shocking collision is sometimes so hard that each animal must stand still for more than a minute to recover from the shock. The rivals continue to ram each other, again and again, until one becomes exhausted or injured, and retreats. The winner postures and preens, then struts away to claim his ewes. In this process of natural selection, the stronger animals are the ones who reproduce the most offspring.

Photo © Daniel J. Cox, Natural Exposures

ELK (WAPITI), *(Cervus elaphus)*

Photo by Carol Polich

ELK (WAPITI)

Photo by Stan Osolinski

Photo by Carol Polich

ELK

Photo by Nancy Sanford

BULL MOOSE, *(Alces alces)*

MOOSE

Photo by Stan Osolinski

MULE DEER, *(Odocoileus hemionus)*

MULE DEER

WHITE-TAILED DEER

Photo © Daniel J. Cox, Natural Exposures

BISON, *(Bison bison)*

Photo by Carol Polich

BISON

Photo by Stan Osolinski

PRONGHORN ANTELOPE, *(Antilocapra americana)*

Photo by Carol Polich

Photo by Carol Polich

PRONGHORN ANTELOPE

Photo by Carol Polich

MOUNTAIN (BIGHORN) SHEEP, *(Ovis canadensis)*

Photo by Ron Sanford

MOUNTAIN (BIGHORN) SHEEP

Photo by Stan Osolinski

MOUNTAIN GOAT, *(Oreamnos americanus)*

Photo by Richard Strange

CARNIVORES

The flesh-eating mammals serve a specialized function in the wilderness. In nature's grand cycle of checks and balances, each. animal must have its predator. The only predators large enough to hunt and kill big animals, such as bison, moose and elk, are wolves, mountain lions and grizzly bears. These predator populations were greatly depleted during the settlement of the west when ranchers and farmers killed hundreds of thousands of the animals in an effort to save their livestock. The surviving big cats and grizzlies retreated to higher country and are reluctant to hunt in the lower valleys, where they, themselves, may become prey to their only predator, man.

In the mountains south of Canada, the gray wolf disappeared almost entirely. However, in the last half of the 20th century, environmental awareness about the importance of the wolf's ecological role led to wolf restoration programs and the animal was reintroduced to the American Rockies. Small packs now reside in several states.

Foxes, coyotes, and bobcats are cunning and resourceful nocturnal hunters. Their chief food is smaller mammals, such as rodents and rabbits. Coyotes sometimes hunt in packs and have been known to cooperate in killing larger prey such as deer. Often, however, if the food chain is in good balance, smaller carnivores clean up the carcasses left behind by larger predators.

Members of the weasel family, including the playful river otter, are widespread in the mountains and valleys. These predators are seldom seen but are always busy hunting small rodents, birds, frogs, fish and other similar prey to help maintain a natural balance.

GRIZZLY BEAR. *(Llrsus arctos horribilis)*

GRIZZLY BEAR

Photo by Ron Sanford

Photo by Ron Sanford

GRIZZLY BEAR

Photo by Stan Osolinski

BLACK BEAR. *(Ursus americanus)*

Photo © Daniel J. Cox, Natural Exposures

GRAY WOLF, *(Canis lupus)*

Photo © Daniel J. Cox, Natural Exposures

GRAY WOLF

Photo by Ron Sanford

MOUNTAIN LION, *(Puma conocolor)*

COYOTE, *(Canis latrans)*

COYOTE

Photo by Ron Sanford

Photo by Ron Sanford

LYNX, *(Lynx lynx)*

BOBCAT, *(Lynx rufus)*

Photo by Carol Polich

RED FOX, *(Vulpes vulpes)*

Photo by Ron Sanford

Photo by Ron Sanford

BADGER, *(Taxidea taxus)*

Photo © Daniel J. Cox, Natural Exposures

RACCOON, *(Procyon lotor)*

RIVER OTTER, *(Lutra canadensis)*

LONG-TAILED WEASEL, *(Mustela frenata)*

GNAWING MAMMALS

In the hierarchy of hard working mountain animals, gnawing mammals perform their roles with great efficiency. People love to watch squirrels and chipmunks dart out from trees to grab a nut or some other food morsel. These friendly little creatures stand upright to inspect the treat. If the food is approved, the chipmunk tucks it into its bulging cheek and runs off to its burrow to save the treasure for winter.

The stocky prairie dog is an astonishing social animal, but it is a menace to ranchers. The animals live in a social community within an elaborate network of tunnels. Some prairie dog "towns" grow so large that they spread over several miles and house millions of individuals. Because these rodents eat grass, roots, weeds and seeds, farmers killed many over the years and the species became threatened. Unfortunately, the natural predators that might have held the population in check were also being killed, poisoned and run-off. This is another example of ecological imbalance.

One of the most industrious mountain animals is the beaver. This unusual mammal is a master architect and engineer. Uniquely adapted for its dam-building job, the beaver has large curved incisors to cut and fell trees; as well as webbed rear feet and a paddle-shaped tail to assist in swimming. Using ingenuity and extraordinary feats of strength, the beaver cuts, drags and skids logs to the construction site to build a colony of sticks and mud. When the dam has created a pond deep enough not to freeze solidly in winter, the beaver builds underwater entrances to an inside lodge with a nest raised on an upper floor above water. The beaver creates its own environment and a habitat to suit itself. If the dams and ponds continue undisturbed, other wildlife will settle here, and soon, an entire ecosystem evolves.

The gnawing-animal families contain many other members. Among those that are common to the mountains and valleys are rabbits, hare, marmots, pikas and the porcupine. The traits and habitats of most of these animals represent adaptations to protect themselves against predators and cold weather. Many rodents burrow into the ground to create a safe hideaway from their enemies and to protect against winter freezing. Some build a nest around their food cache and hibernate until spring. Each animal has a role to play in nature's four-act drama.

Photo © John Hinde Curteich

PRAIRIE DOG, *(Cynomys ludovicianus)*

Photo by Ron Sanford

PORCUPINE, *(Erethizon dorsatum)*

BEAVER, *(Castor canadensis)*

YELLOW-BELLIED MARMOT, *(Marmota flaviventris)*

Photo by Stan Osolinski

GOLDEN-MANTLED GROUND SQUIRREL, *(Citellus lateralis)*

Photo by Richard Strange

Photo by Stan Osolinski

LEAST CHIPMUNK, *(Tamias minimus)*

Photo by Stan Osolinski

UINTA GROUND SQUIRREL, *(Spermophilus armatus)*

Photo by Richard Strange

ABERT'S SQUIRREL, *(Sciurus aberti)*

Because of abundant fish-filled waters and fields of seed-producing plants, birds thrive in the mountains. Over 200 species have been identified in the Rockies. Each bird, big or small, has its part to play in the ecosystem.

reports that "one packed Ponderosa Pine was studded with an estimated 50,000 acorns." A food cache of such abundance is an example of the hard work and diligence that nature expects of her creatures. Those who work, eat. Other western favorites are members

*W*indswept and weathered, the forest stands, proud and secure.... *In bold grandeur, endows, rest and refuge among evergreen boughs....* *Home and hotel to a million living things.*

...Lucy Hanley

Photo by Stan Osolinski

Lush forests lakes and streams provide excellent habitat for birds. Among the mountain regulars are water birds, including mallards, coots, loons, geese, gulls, swans and blue herons. Some of these birds are temporary visitors that have flown from great distances. Few sights in nature are so stirring as that of a flock of rare white trumpeter swans, with wingspans up to 7 feet, arrowing across the sky, traveling from the tundra to the breeding grounds, honking their clamorous musical calls. Equally thrilling is an occasional sighting of the great blue heron, standing 4 feet tall, wading in freshwater marshes to catch fish, frogs and snakes. Perching nearby may be a double crested cormorant watching silently as gulls, terns, pelicans, and other surface fishers skim over the water seeking food. From a high branch on a Lodgepole Pine or the top of a nearby dead tree, an eagle, osprey or hawk may plunge into the water to scoop up a fish to take back to its nest to feed its young.

Within the forests are many small perching birds, including sparrows, robins, larks, jays, bluebirds, blackbirds and numerous other colorful varieties, including songbirds. Here, birds hunt insects and scatter seeds. A woodpecker keeps busy hammering a tree trunk, seeking bugs, or drilling holes to store acorns. North American Wildlife by Reader's Digest (1982)

of the grouse family whose traditional dancing courtship rites, including rhythmic wing-drumming displays, are unique frenzied spectacles.

One of the world's main bird migration routes is the Central Flyway, which follows the line of the Rocky Mountains. Generally, birds migrate because snow and ice make it hard for them to find food. Many migratory birds stop along their way in the lakes and forests of the Rockies. Some stay only long enough to eat and rest, while others become permanent residents. Because of many bird sanctuaries along this well-traveled course, birds are able to rest, feed and breed without being disturbed by man.

BALD EAGLE. *(Haliaeetus leucocephalus)*

Photo © Daniel J. Cox, Natural Exposures

BALD EAGLE

Photo by Ron Sanford

GOLDEN EAGLE. *(Aquila chrysaetos)*

Photo © Daniel J. Cox, Natural Exposures

GREAT GRAY OWL, *(Strix nebu losa)*

Photo by Richard Strange

OSPREY, *(Pandion haliaetus)*

Photo by Stan Osolinski

RAVEN, *(Corvus corax)*

Photo by Stan Osolinski

YELLOW-HEADED BLACKBIRD, *(Agelaius icterocephalus)*

STELLAR JAY, *(Cyanocitta stelleri)*

Photo by Stan Osolinski

WHITE PELICAN, *(Pelecanus erythrorhynchos)*

TRUMPETER SWANS, *(Cygnus cygnus)*

Photo by Carol Polich

CANADIAN GEESE, *(Branta canadensis)*

Photo by Stan Osolinski

Photo by Richard Strange

CANADIAN GEESE

Photo by Carol Polich

MALLARD DUCKS, *(Anas platyrhynchos)*

RUFFED GROUSE, *(Bonasa umbrellus)*

BLUE GROUSE, *(Dendragapus obscurus)*

Photo by Richard Strange

WILD TURKEY (MALE), *(Meleagris gallopavo)*

MOUNTAIN BLUEBIRD, *(Sialia currucoides)*

Photo by Stan Osolinski

WHITE-TAILED PTARMIGAN, *(Lagopus leucurus)*

Photo by Carol Polich

SANDHILL CRANE, *(Grus canadensis)*